YOU ARE THE SPELL

MEDITATIONS FOR A MAGICAL LIFE

T. THORN COYLE

Copyright © 2023 by T. Thorn Coyle
Cover Design © 2023 by T. Thorn Coyle
Cover Art and Interior Images
© 2023 by Maxine Miller

Paperback ISBN: 978-1-946476-49-4

All Rights Reserved. No part of this book may be used—including but not limited to—the training of, or use by, artificial intelligence or reproduced in any form or by any electronic or mechanical means, including information storage and retrieval systems, without written permission from the author, except for the use of brief quotations in a book review.

CONTENTS

PART I
OPENING

1. Cast Yourself — 3
2. About This Book — 4
3. How to Use This Book — 6
4. Assessment — 8
5. What is Important? — 12

PART II
BLESSING

6. Blessing Your Feet — 15
7. Blessing Your Hands — 16
8. Blessing Your Lungs — 17
9. Blessing Your Heart — 18
10. Blessing Your Mind — 19
11. Blessing Your Senses — 21

PART III
BUILDING

12. Bone — 25
13. Bone Meditation One — 28
14. Bone Meditation Two — 31
15. Bone Meditation Three — 33
16. Bone Meditation Four — 35
17. Bone Meditation Five — 37
18. Bone Meditation Six — 39
19. Bone Meditation Seven — 41
20. Bone Meditation Eight — 43
21. Bone Meditation Nine — 45

22. Bone Meditation Ten	47
23. The Ritual of Building	49

PART IV
CENTERING

24. Crystal	53
25. Crystal Meditation One	55
26. Crystal Meditation Two	58
27. Crystal Meditation Three	60
28. Crystal Meditation Four	63
29. Crystal Meditation Five	65
30. Crystal Meditation Six	67
31. Crystal Meditation Seven	69
32. Crystal Meditation Eight	71
33. Crystal Meditation Nine	73
34. Crystal Meditation Ten	75
The Ritual of Centering	77

PART V
WISHING

35. Dandelion	81
36. Dandelion Meditation One	84
37. Dandelion Meditation Two	86
38. Dandelion Meditation Three	88
39. Dandelion Meditation Four	90
40. Dandelion Meditation Five	92
41. Dandelion Meditation Six	94
42. Dandelion Meditation Seven	96
43. Dandelion Meditation Eight	98
44. Dandelion Meditation Nine	100
45. Dandelion Meditation Ten	102
46. The Ritual of Wishing	104

PART VI
DECIDING

47. Blade — 109
48. Blade Meditation One — 112
49. Blade Meditation Two — 114
50. Blade Meditation Three — 116
51. Blade Meditation Four — 118
52. Blade Meditation Five — 121
53. Blade Meditation Six — 123
54. Blade Meditation Seven — 125
55. Blade Meditation Eight — 127
56. Blade Meditation Nine — 129
57. Blade Meditation Ten — 131
58. The Ritual of Deciding — 133

PART VII
MANIFESTING

59. Bee — 139
60. Bee Meditation One — 142
61. Bee Meditation Two — 144
62. Bee Meditation Three — 146
63. Bee Meditation Four — 148
64. Bee Meditation Five — 150
65. Bee Meditation Six — 152
66. Bee Meditation Seven — 154
67. Bee Meditation Eight — 156
68. Bee Meditation Nine — 158
69. Bee Meditation Ten — 160
70. The Ritual of Manifestation — 162

PART VIII
CLOSING

71. The Cycle Continues — 167

Thank You	169
Reviews	171
About the Author	173
Also by T. Thorn Coyle	175

PART I

OPENING

1

CAST YOURSELF

Cast yourself; you are the spell....

What would it feel like if you treated those words as true?

What would be required for you to believe in yourself more than you believe in the stories others tell? Or even in the stories you tell yourself? The ones you've carried, perhaps for years?

Spend some time in contemplation. Take a conscious breath. Be present with yourself and the world.

2

ABOUT THIS BOOK

The meditations within these pages come directly from my own morning sitting practice and my daily walking meditations. When I realized these meditations were keys to my own continued magical unfolding, I decided to share them.

I began first by sharing them on social media, alongside photos I took on my walks. The response was quiet, yet tremendous. Person after person wrote me privately to say how much those simple posts were helping them, day to day.

So I was called to write more, and to expand and deepen these simple meditations into something anyone could work with over time.

These meditations have been a gift from my own

guides and that quiet inner voice that arises when I center and pay attention.

I hope that they will also become gifts in your life, coaxing your own inner guidance to the surface.

We can all live more magical lives, regardless of our conditions. We can continuously return to noticing, then move into building, centering, wishing, deciding...once done, manifestation becomes easier. We center, decide, and invoke our will and wisdom.

Then we act.

A candle is lit. The magic of our lives is in motion.

3

HOW TO USE THIS BOOK

This is a book for dreamers and builders, manifestors and deciders, meditators and magic-makers....

You can use it as an oracle, enacting the ancient art of bibliomancy. Breathe and center yourself, close your eyes, then find a page. Whatever is on that page is your meditation for the day or the week.

You can also use this book to guide your daily meditations. The opening is a self-blessing ritual. Each section thereafter guides us through a sequence from Bone: Building, to Crystal: Centering, Dandelion: Wishing, to Blade: Deciding, and finally to Bee: Manifesting.

Some say that it takes at least twenty-one days to

form a habit. How about two months? What might shift after two full cycles of the moon?

Let the meditations and practices here become useful spiritual gifts, drawing you into a place of daily contemplation, and deepening your sense of connection to yourself and your desires over time. Will you commit to gifting yourself this time every day?

How might your life change if you did?

Another use for this book is in close relationships. Pick a page with a friend, partner, or other loved one, and talk about what feelings or ideas it sparks in you. How does it connect to you personally, and to your relationship?

You can also use the book to spark community conversations! Use it to center everyone at the start of a meeting. Pick a page to read aloud as a way to slow down as a family before a meal.

In other words: this book is designed for you, and your life. This book is designed to unlock your deeper wisdom and expand your magic.

Use it as you will.

Cast yourself. You are the spell.

4

ASSESSMENT

We begin with an assessment, and being present with ourselves.

I : *Adjust your body, still your mind.*

Sit down. Adjust your knees and your spine. Adjust your head and your neck. Shrug your shoulders up, then down. Slow your breathing. Find your center, that still place between your navel and your pelvic bowl. Imagine you can drop your attention into that cauldron.

Breathe. And breathe. And breathe again.

II: *What in you feels broken?*

What in you feels broken? What feels small, or tired, or frightened, or shattered, or scattered, or alone?

Find that place inside of you. Where does this feeling live in your body? Or your mind?

Feel those small, tender places.

Say: "I don't know if everything is going to be okay. But I do know that there is love to be had and beauty to encounter. I do know you are wanted here. You are necessary. You are part of life itself. I will breathe with you. I will hold you. I will comfort you, and we will get through all of this together."

III: *What in you feels content and whole?*

Breathe. Feel your belly. Your chest. Your feet. Your arms.

Breathe. Let your emotions surface. Feel the edges of your skin.

Breathe.

What in you feels content? What parts of your life feel as if they are going well? What is something you currently enjoy? What parts of you feel healthy, flexible, strong, or whole?

Who you are, as you are, you are complete in this

moment. Even any longing or distress are part of this completion.

Do you feel whole, right now? Or can you allow yourself to feel whole? And if not all of you, breathe into that place where contentment resides.

And breathe.

IV: *What do you want or need?*

Are your basic needs getting met, emotionally, physically, mentally, financially, creatively?

Is there something else you need?

What about want? What do you want right now? Ample time? More love? More creativity? Enough money? To be heard? To be seen?

Write down your wants and needs. How does that feel? Breathe.

What is one small thing you can shift—right now—to address one of your wants or needs?

V: *What do you desire?*

What do you desire? What is your strongest wish in this moment, right now? Can you feel it? Can you touch it? Can you see it, hear it, or taste it?

Invite your desire, your wish, to come closer.

Hold out your arms. Embrace your wish. Hold your desire.

Breathe with it.

Then let it go, and see what happens.

VI: *Invoke the sacred.*

What Gods, Goddesses, Powers, or Guidance do you call upon? Do you call upon the spirits of place? Of Holy Nature? Do you call upon the intelligences that reside in the unseen realms? Do you invoke Mystery?

Whatever connects you to the worlds outside the edges of your physical body, do so now.

Speak your prayers into form.

5

WHAT IS IMPORTANT?

Take a breath.
Think of one thing that is important to you.
What will you do to honor that this week?

PART II

BLESSING

6

BLESSING YOUR FEET

Notice your feet.

Think of all the places you have gone with them.

Bless your feet this week. Thank them for being a part of you. Bless any ambulatory devices you use, too. Every day, notice what your feet or mobility devices do with and for you.

"I give thanks to the feet that carry me. I bless their shape, their form, their flexibility and their pain. I bless the rough and smooth. The weakness and strength. Blessed be my feet."

7

BLESSING YOUR HANDS

Notice your hands.

Think of all they have touched, or held, or worked on.

Bless your hands this week. Thank them for being a part of you. Notice them every day, at work, play, and rest.

"I give thanks to these hands that push and pull. That hold and open. I bless their ability to work and to play. I bless their flexibility and their pain. I bless the rough and smooth. The weakness and strength. Blessed be my hands."

8

BLESSING YOUR LUNGS

Notice your lungs.

Think of the air they move, in and through and out of the rest of your body.

Bless your lungs this week. No matter what condition they are in, bless them for being a part of you. Every day, spend time noticing the movement of your lungs.

"I give thanks to these lungs that draw in and release. That move oxygen through my body, and release gases outward. I bless their ability and their weakness. I bless the deep inhalation of ease and the sharpness that comes with pain. Blessed be my lungs."

9

BLESSING YOUR HEART

Notice your heart.

Think of the blood it pumps and circulates, day after day after day.

Bless your heart this week. Thank it for being a part of you and helping to keep you alive.

"I give thanks to my heart that pumps blood through my veins. I bless its steady drumbeat and its faltering rhythms. I bless its ability to keep constricting and releasing, despite the strain of life. I bless heartbreak and wholeness. Blessed be my heart."

10

BLESSING YOUR MIND

Notice your mind.

Notice your thoughts as they ebb and flow.

Think of your brain. Think of its folds and ripples. Its synapses firing.

Bless your mind this week. Thank your brain for being a part of you. Thank your imagination and the worlds it opens up inside you. Thank the ways in which your mind functions, assessing the world around you.

If you have trouble with your brain—fog from chronic physical illness, mental health challenges, or issues from injury—find ways to honor that, too. Honor how your brain works, whether neurotypical or neurodivergent.

"I give thanks for my mind and my brain. I bless its abilities, its quirks, and its uniqueness. I bless the folds and ripples. I bless my imagination and my rationality. Blessed be my mind."

11

BLESSING YOUR SENSES

Notice your senses: taste, touch, sight, hearing, smell.

Think of all the information and connection your senses open up for you.

Bless your senses this week. Thank them for being a part of you. Bless any assistive devices you use, too: glasses, hearing aids, or other tools. Every day, notice what your senses do with and for the rest of you.

"I give thanks to the senses that connect me to the world. I bless my eyes, ears, tongue, nose, and skin. I bless the subtle and the intense, and the ability to better perceive. Blessed be my senses."

PART III
BUILDING

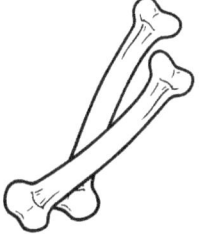

12

BONE

Our bones are part of our foundation. They are the structure from which the rest of our body hangs. Our bones provide scaffolding for muscle and tendon, and a safe place for our heart, brain, and lungs. Bones enable us to move through the world. The state of our bones affects our relationship with the world around us.

Sure, we could have begun talking of building with one cell. Cells are also building blocks of our lives. But bones? We have a better idea of how they function in our lives, and how they literally form structure.

So, for this book at least, we begin with bone.

We begin with building.

What is the structure of your life? How much space exists within that structure to accommodate play, good health, rest, exploration, spiritual practice, community, creativity, and magic?

What parts of your current structure support you? What parts of your structure constrict you in ways that no longer serve?

Take some time and ponder this. Perhaps write some things down.

Then ask: How would I like to change my structure? What can I keep and what might I let go?

You can ask the same questions about the structure of your closest relationships, and expand out to include your communities.

Building is a process. Building takes time, attention, intention, and resources. That said, we always begin where we are, not in some perfect future. We build one block or nail, breath or vision at a time.

This section on building is designed to help us reorient ourselves to attend to the things we truly want to build.

We want building to be sustainable, flexible, and open for more growth or contraction as needed.

To build, we tune in with the cycles of life itself. The turning of the tides. The change of the seasons. The shift from day to night and back again.

To build, we think of the finch or crow, selecting twigs and grasses for their nests.

To build, we think of ants and bees, working together.

To build, we think of hills, and plains, and mountains. The bones of the earth.

To build, we take a breath. We adjust our spines.

And we begin....

13

BONE MEDITATION ONE

I am one with this place, this ecosystem, this city, this time. I am one with earth and sky.

No matter where we live, we are part of a local ecosystem. Whether a city, a town, a village, a forest, or on the edge of an ocean or field, we are affected by everything around us, and we affect our world in turn.

Our local ecosystem is part of a larger, regional ecosystem. Which is part of even larger systems, still. And our home planet, Earth, is part of a solar system.... On and on it goes.

We are a part of life and death, creativity and change. So, how do we acknowledge this?

One day on a walk, I came across a large wooden utility pole. It was festooned with bright beads and crow feathers. People in the neighborhood had turned it into an ersatz altar, an echo of an ancient God Pole, erected on a sidewalk in a medium-sized Pacific Northwest city. My writer's mind—and my pagan mind—immediately began to form a story about the people gathering to honor something sacred together.

And perhaps that is true, though I'm fairly certain that the beads and feathers were added by different people, over time, who had never met or discussed building this little pocket of sacred art and being.

But the collection of feathers and beads marked the building of community, nonetheless. Consciously or not, picking up a dropped feather and placing it, shaft first, to decorate a pole is still ritualized action. It is action out of the ordinary stream of life.

Those people, through pausing and choosing to decorate this pole, connected with me, however many months or weeks we were separated by time. I paused to appreciate the handiwork of those who came before.

In that small way, we build the neighborhood together.

What rituals connect you to place? What roots you in the sacred? What reminds you that you are part of the bones of the earth and the building blocks of time?

14

BONE MEDITATION TWO

Practice makes possible.

PRACTICING MAKES THINGS POSSIBLE. We practice spiritual disciplines. We study magic. We practice being with other humans, animals, or Powers That Be. We practice learning something new.

Conscious repetition builds both skill and connection. There are many ways to practice fruitful, nourishing repetition, and over time, this helps us to replace unconscious repetitions that only serve to disconnect us.

We build our relationship to practice through

small actions of intention: We light a candle. Straighten our spines. Breathe in silence, gazing at the candle flame. We take a conscious drink of water, connecting with the life-bringing liquid on our tongue, and rolling down our throat.

But sometimes we resist practice. We resist learning something new. It's hard to put ourselves out there. It can feel hard to show up. It can also feel deeply satisfying. Sometimes we are not only up for the challenge, we crave it.

Without practice, nothing intentional can happen. With practice, positive changes—incremental or large—happen all the time.

What is your current relationship with practice? What is your relationship with learning? Are you willing to try and fail? Are you willing to try and succeed?

Are you willing to practice, to devote energy and time to something?

Are you willing to build upon something, piece by piece, moment by moment?

Are you willing to invoke change?

15

BONE MEDITATION THREE

We can be both delicate and strong. *Resilient and beautiful.*

IN ORDER TO build a strong foundation, it is helpful to know ourselves. And that means taking stock of all of the parts of ourselves. Not just the parts we like or dislike. Not just the parts others see. Our secret parts, too. Our past. Our present. Our possible future.

To build, we need to not just be one thing or another. Denying parts of ourselves weakens us over time. Does this mean we let our less helpful-seeming parts run the show? No. But ignoring those parts of self usually means they're steering things from underground. Better to assess who we truly are and move from there, than pretend to some false perfection.

We can embrace all of our facets, and bring them to the task. This is important for us as individuals, and also to us in community. A group made up of only one type of person is like a garden with only one type of plant, or a building made only of nails.

Strength arises from diversity.

We contain multitudes, as the poet said. This not only makes us more interesting, it makes us more resilient, and capable of greater depths of compassion and connection.

By embracing more of ourselves, we can embrace greater diversity around us, and that helps us all.

Be delicate. Be strong. Embrace your beauty. Become resilient.

Then allow the world around you to do the same.

16

BONE MEDITATION FOUR

*hat feeds me right now? How do I help feed others?*

WHAT IS FEEDING you right now?

Is it good food? Music? Art? Books? Friendship? Exercise? Rest?

It is important to take care of ourselves and each other. We need rejuvenation in order to find renewal.

Humans need music. We need art. We need stories. We need conversation. We need rest. We need a connection to trees, water, and sky.

Humans need hope. A sense that life can thrive

even during difficult times. There is magic in a hope grounded in the reality that difficulty is not all that makes up the world.

Hope does not need to be large or grandiose. As a matter of fact, I take more solace in small doses of hope than in the large. The small things feel more real to me. More manageable.

Some days, making breakfast to nourish our bodies is an act of hope.

Some days, making breakfast can even become an act of defiance. Making breakfast, eating breakfast—and maybe even having the good fortune to share that breakfast—tells a harsh, punitive society:

"I don't care what you do to me. Today, I choose to live."

Every time we feed ourselves—with whatever it is—we choose to live. Every meal prepared, and every song or story shared, is a commitment to nourish ourselves and each other.

We say, "Not today, despair and death. Not today."

Invoking hope through action builds the world we want to inhabit. And when we invoke hope as conscious magic? Our actions triple in power.

17

BONE MEDITATION FIVE

The poet's ivy clings, that's how it grows.
 Sometimes we must hold tight; sometimes, let go...

TO BUILD REQUIRES both holding fast and surrendering. Yes, we need a plan. Yes, like ivy, we need tenacity. But to build well also requires releasing attachment. Ivy, clinging too tightly, can choke out other life. Ivy, clinging too tightly, can eventually tear a building down.

The same happens with us when we become too attached to how growth and building look, and to what we think the outcome ought to be.

The outcome is never what we think it ought to

be at first, because—as I always say—as soon as we move or act, the future changes. We need to co-create the future with what we are building. We need to co-create the future with people and circumstances around us.

Some days, yes, we must hold fast! We must be tenacious. We must dig deep and reach and not give up.

Other days? We need a deeper breath. Sometimes in order to build, we must let go.

Where are you in this process today? Is there something you have been too quick to let go of? Or something you need to release close attachment to?

What will best help you shift and build, and give you room to grow?

18

BONE MEDITATION SIX

One day, you realized your wounds helped you to heal.

WE ALL HAVE wounds from the past. Some of us are continuously wounded in the present. If you are that latter person, what changes can you make to stop the wounding and begin to heal?

A teacher of mine used to ask people who came to him for help, "Do you want to be healed of this?" Sometimes we must invoke compassion and ask ourselves that question, too.

But often? Even though they have left us with scars, we are ready to move on from the wounds of the past. Just like a tree grows a callous over a wound, allowing it to put its energy toward new growth instead of constant pain, we too make space for something new.

Our wounds—once recognized—offer us wisdom that we never had before. We can build from that. We can learn to ask for help sometimes. We learn that we don't need to do it all alone. As a matter of fact, we cannot do it all alone.

And that recognition helps to build friendship and community. We ask for help and offer help in turn.

Together, we come to realize that even if everything is not always okay, life burgeons anyway. Moss grows. Insects build. Bones re-knit. Cells grow.

Life insists on life. Are you willing to heal? Are you willing to nurture new growth despite your pain?

19

BONE MEDITATION SEVEN

Some days, we need a good stretch....

WHAT IN YOU needs a good stretch right now? Your body? Your emotions? Your ambitions? Your mind?

Building requires flexibility. Without flexibility, the strongest things end up brittle, bound up. This weakens systems, people, and relationships over time. Without flexibility, there is no resilience. No reserves to draw upon. Little ability to bounce back, because frankly, the more rigid an object becomes, the less room there is to bounce.

So I ask again: What in your life needs to stretch

right now? Is it your relationship to work or creativity? Your interpersonal relationships? Your community vision?

Does your imagination need to stretch itself? Have you gotten so bound up in your current systems that you've forgotten to make room for outside input or more flow?

What feels bound up?

Pause a moment. Notice. Breathe. Are there knots that need loosening? In what facets of your life? Examine this question from as many angles as you can today. But don't tense up around it. Engage with a sense of curiosity and openness.

Start with stretching your body. Then figure out some ways to stretch your heart and mind.

20

BONE MEDITATION EIGHT

The world is filled with geometry: triangles and building blocks. What is my piece?

WHAT HELPS YOU BUILD? How do you help others build? What is your piece of the geometric puzzle that exists all around us?

Cooperation is a geometry. Just as we cannot build alone, we cannot hold things together on our own. We may think we can, and tell ourselves the story that we can, but that is not true.

Ever.

To build a house, we need trees, or sand and gravel, or glass. We need someone to plane the boards. We need someone to have fired brick. We need tools to mix concrete. Even if we are starting from scratch, so to speak, and making all of our own tools, and doing every speck of work ourselves, the natural world itself is working with us.

The same principles apply to relationships, creativity, businesses, spiritual groups, and life itself.

There are no "self-made" people.

We all help make each other, every day.

We work in the geometry of life, forming triangles, and squares, and circles together.

What might help you to remember this? And can you call upon some allies to help with what is currently in front of you?

We build with the shapes of our lives.

21

BONE MEDITATION NINE

Today is a good day to share what you have and ask for what you need.

NOT ONE THING in our cosmos exists without impacting and being impacted by everything around it. Everything in the cosmos shares what it has with everything else.

Mutual Aid is the rock-bottom, unshakeable knowledge that we are all in this life together and must share what skills and goods we have in order to survive and thrive.

This is not a one-to-one exchange. This is not

quid pro quo. There is no keeping track or keeping score.

Mutual Aid is the flow of gifts throughout community. One day I need help; another day, you need help. One day I have something to offer. Another day you have something to offer. We all have skills and talents to share. You might give to one person and ask for help from yet another. And that is how it works. Mutual Aid builds functional, healthy community systems.

We offer what we have and ask for what we need. We build a world—and a community—together.

Crows, squirrels, humans, beavers, wolves, gulls, plants, stars, planets, watersheds, clouds, and trees... there is nothing that exists outside these cycles of life that knit us together into one beautiful, radiant whole.

22

BONE MEDITATION TEN

Blessings for the living and the dead. All things transform.

THE BONES of what came before help us build what is yet to come.

Composted leaves and vegetables. The bones of trees and stone. Innovation and invention. The spark from an old idea. A snatch of music or poetry. Our ancestors of spirit and blood family. The change of seasons...

The living and the dying work in concert with each other, making space for what is yet to come.

The caterpillar turns into goo, and somehow

remakes itself into a butterfly. The butterfly struggles to emerge from its shell. That struggle itself gives it the strength to fly. We ourselves arise from the shadows of our former selves, carrying the past with us as we formulate the future in the now.

We live with what was, is, and shall be. We live with grief and pain and loss. We live with love and joy and promise. We live with all things seen and unseen. We live inside multiple worlds, and dying stars live inside the iron of our blood.

How beautiful. How magical. How astounding.

We can learn to bless it all.

23

THE RITUAL OF BUILDING

For this ritual, you will need an object that represents foundation, stability, or building. It could be a stone, a stick, an image of a house, an image of community, a piece of honeycomb...let your intuition guide you.

You will also want a candle and a cup of water.

I often like to tidy or clean before doing ritual, allowing the preparation of my space to prepare me internally, as well. This is up to you.

Place your objects together wherever you have clear space. If you have a dedicated working altar, that is perfect. If you don't? Any surface can become a temporary altar space.

Slow your breathing down. Adjust your posture.

Relax. Close your eyes for a few moments and just breathe and be.

Next, light your candle. Look at or pick up the object or image that represents building and foundation to you. Breathe with that. Enter into the rock or stone, the stick, the honeycomb, or the image....

What does it have to tell you about the power of building? Let the object whisper to your intuition. Feel where the information resonates in your physical body.

Now, think of your current want, need, or desire around building and foundation. Let this fill you, from your bones outward.

What is one thing you can do to activate the power of building in your life, right now?

Lift your object or image and swirl it over the candle flame. Speak that activation out loud. "I will.... I activate the power of Building."

Set the object back down on the altar. Thank the object. Extinguish the candle. Drink some water. Take some time to simply be.

You are now ready to move into the power of centering.

PART IV
CENTERING

24

CRYSTAL

Crystals grow in clusters, deep inside the womb of the earth. They reach in the safety of still caves. Once brought to light, cracked open, they shimmer with an otherworldly light.

Like a crystal cave, there is a place of stillness inside you. It does not matter what chaos swirls inside or around you, this stillness abides.

Slow your breathing down. Focus on the air moving into and out of your lungs. Notice the natural pause that occurs between each inhalation and exhalation.

Drop into that pause. Allow that space to expand around you. Keep dropping until your attention rests somewhere between your navel and pelvic bowl.

This is where your inner stillness resides. And from this place of stillness, wisdom rises.

By centering every morning—breathing into that space between the navel and the pelvic bowl—we set the template for our day. We remind our cells and our consciousness that there is a core part of us that does not need to rush frantically through our lives, avoiding or seeking, desperate, angry, worried, stressed, or afraid.

Things arise or fall. Other things take their place. We greet the world with a strong sense of self, and a core both flexible and strong.

Balance shifts and moves, and we move with it, around our central core.

By connecting to the stillness at our core, we breathe more easily, and our attention grows more acute and less fractured over time. Intuition increases. Serendipity happens more often. Our spells are more successful. Doors open that we may not have noticed before.

Centering becomes the essence of our being. Life appears—pulsing with magic—and we are present to greet what may come.

CRYSTAL MEDITATION ONE

*ay time be gentle with us as we change.*

CHANGE IS INEVITABLE. Sometimes we race toward it, ready for something new. Other times we fight or fear change. Breathe with it all. Stroke a fingertip across your breastbone. Be gentle with yourself, whether the change feels good or difficult. Allow yourself to shift with what shall be.

We ask that time be gentle with us because there is no stopping change. We can learn to embrace it—even in what feels like a headlong rush—and from our centered place, we can breathe and slow down inside.

That lessens the impact of change. It becomes no less significant but less brutal as we recalibrate and adjust ourselves to the fact that change is coming. Keep breathing. Put a hand on your belly and a hand on your heart and feel how your body expands and contracts. As the air moves in and out of mouth and nose and lungs, you can be gentle on yourself. The gentler you are the gentler the world can be.

Think of building physical strength. The harder you go at it from the start, the longer your muscles take to recover. But if you ease in to building strength, adding one small weight at a time, one extra block to your walk, your muscles grow and expand with you. And with the shift, the body meets the change instead of the change running over the body.

The same is true of hearts and minds. Can you learn one thing today instead of trying to cram in ten?

Gentleness supports centeredness. Gentleness supports resilience. Gentleness supports increased strength over time.

Not everything has to be full-out, though sometimes that's our ambition and our wish. And sometimes that's appropriate, even satisfying.

So how do you decide? When do you need more gentleness? When do you need to increase the pace or the pressure?

Cultivating the ability to be gentle enables us to make these choices. That way, when it's time to work full-out, we have a greater ability to do so because our reserves aren't spent and we haven't overburdened ourselves.

Center yourself in gentleness today and see what happens.

26

CRYSTAL MEDITATION TWO

*E*verything *in nature has a pattern, whether we can perceive it clearly or not.*

BREATHE IN. What patterns do you notice around you?

Breathe out. What patterns do you notice in your life?

Everything in nature has a pattern.

We often try to center ourselves in sameness. We think that if everything is always the same, it will be perfect. We can think that perfection is the only thing that's going to help us with our own stability.

But in nature, not only does everything have a pattern, everything cycles, and cycles mean flux.

So, to center ourselves we must remember that we, too, are a pattern and our lives are patterns. We too, cycle and our lives are in flux. We can consistently return to center.

Noticing the patterns of our days helps us to center more easily. Noticing the patterns of our years helps us recognize our own cycles and center within and around those.

Life is not static. Centering is not static. We breathe with the cosmos and the trees. We root and we rise. We reflect sunlight and shadow. We change like the leaves. We unfold like the petals of a flower. We flow like ocean waves or desert winds.

Notice the patterns in your life and breathe.

27

CRYSTAL MEDITATION THREE

There is eternity in a single drop of rain....

CRYSTALS FORM SLOWLY, over time.

Liquid cools and hardens. Atoms coalesce. Crystals shape themselves, forming facets and striations. Deep underground, pressed by the earth itself, over time, impurities only make these clusters more beautiful.

What helps you slow down? What helps you expand along with time?

The ancient Egyptians had a concept of time that shifted according to light and dark time of year. The hours of the day were the same in number, but within those markers, time within the hours of day and night shifted in length according to season and where the sun was in the sky.

In my mind, this always feels as if, for the ancient Egyptians, time breathed, expanding and contracting with the amount of light in the sky.

What helps you breathe with time? Do you slow down in the darker months? Do you do more in the lighter months? Or do you keep time with a mechanical clock regulating your life by external shoulds and should nots?

There is nothing that says we must adhere to mechanized time except for jobs that are often not very well suited to humans. So if we hold one of those jobs, how do we adjust?

We adjust our other activities and our expectations of ourselves, our family members, and our friends. It's all right to say no to things during the darker months. It's all right to say yes during the lighter…or perhaps it's the opposite for you. That's okay too.

There is no need to adjust your life completely to others' expectations. You can expand with time. You can slow down when you need to. But first, you must listen to your heart, body, and soul. What do you want? What do you need? Breathe. Still yourself. Find your center and explore what it means to be you.

Remember there is eternity in a single drop of rain.

CRYSTAL MEDITATION FOUR

Sometimes in order to move, we must remain perfectly still.

IMAGINE A POWERFUL WIND, rushing and howling, battering windows and setting wind chimes to clanging.

Leaves dance in circles, following the pathways of the wind.

Imagine your hands, tucked around a warm cup of tea. Acknowledge yourself as safe and warm, though others are not.

Breathing in and out, grateful for the quiet

moment within the maelstrom. Settle into your center. Allow this sense of well-being to expand.

Now recall the last time you were outside in a great wind. Did it blow hot, or icy cold? Did it steal your breath? Make you laugh? Did it pull and push, tugging and shoving like an insistent dog?

Imagine a wind wrapping around you, as you sit or stand, perfectly still, despite its pushing and tugging. Allow this wind to sweep away your worries and cares. Allow this wind to cleanse you, leaving you refreshed, solid, centered, and feeling alive.

Allow this imaginary wind to rush through your energy fields, making space for what is yet to come.

Sometimes in order to move, we must remain still, no matter what buffets or tries to distract us. Sometimes, in order to grow, we need to become clear.

We have to know what our relationship is to both the inner and outer landscape. We have to learn how to work with our lives, both with our preferences and challenges.

Some days? Yes. We have to walk into the wind. But other days?

We need to stop fighting so hard and just stand still.

We might even find ourselves dancing.

29

CRYSTAL MEDITATION FIVE

There is beauty where you are. Beauty exists where we notice it.

GAZE into the crystal of your life. What do you see?

How often do you pause to notice what is within and around you?

Pausing and noticing is a primary part of my current spiritual practice. Pausing and noticing engages me as an animist and pagan, a magic worker and witch. Pausing and noticing connects me to all that is, and reminds me that I am in an active relationship with the world.

I breathe, and look again. I breathe, and listen. I

breathe.... I remember that this world is worth every breath.

Do all your moments rush one into the other in a frantic movement? Are you barely able to take a breath? If yes, this throws you off center.

Pause right now and take in a conscious breath. Savor this moment.

What do you smell? What do you taste? What do you touch? What do you hear? What do your eyes light upon? Feel this moment in your whole body. Feel this moment in your whole being.

This moment is eternal. And right now, so are you.

What's coming from this center into place? What dawns on the horizon? What lives in the corners of your awareness, dancing at the edges?

In those spaces dwell possibility and renewal.

When we pause, life is reflected back to us. We re-center with the world.

30

CRYSTAL MEDITATION SIX

In order to be kind to ourselves, we must make space to perceive our lives.

SOMETIMES WE NEED TO PAUSE, inhale deeply, and ask what we really want or need. In order to be kind to ourselves, we have to make at least a small amount of space to perceive what is really going on in our lives.

Kindness can look like taking a break. Reading a book. Going for a walk. Eating something nourishing. Kindness can look like pushing ourselves to do the hard thing. Rising to the challenge. Believing we can do it. Kindness can look like having the necessary conversation. Taking a nap. Doing our laundry. Reaching for our dreams.

We need kindness in our communities, too, of course. And frankly, with all the storms going on in the world right now? Most of us are—believe it or not—predisposed to be kind to one another. We care about each other and this world.

A consistent return to center helps us remember to act kindly. This does not necessarily look *nice*, either. I'm not speaking of niceness here, at all. Kindness is linked with empathy and compassion and the understanding that we don't always comprehend the landscapes of our lives. And when we apply kindness to ourselves, we can remember that we are works in progress, and that sometimes the parts of self we grow impatient or frustrated with are the very parts we need to help us live.

We are as we are. Life unfolds. We make our magic from where we are, not from where we think we ought to be.

Take a chance today. Perceive yourself as you really are.

31

CRYSTAL MEDITATION SEVEN

*ach day, there is a sunrise, and the promise of life yet to come.*

CAN YOU APPRECIATE THIS MOMENT, no matter where you are? No matter the time of day or year? Can you feel what is on the horizon? Close your eyes for a moment, and just be.

There is beauty where you are. It doesn't matter if you are in a city alleyway. On a hospital ward. In a garden. At a concert. Spending time with friends. In an office. Working outside in brutal heat or cold. In anger, grief, or joy.

Pause one moment. Center. Breathe. Notice one

thing that is beautiful right now. One thing, large or small. Notice that beautiful thing: a sound, a scent, a sight, a touch, a taste. Breathe it in. Soften your edges and expand.

Let that beauty fill you. Let that beauty cascade down your shoulder blades and into your fingertips. Let that beauty flow like a river down to your toes and up to the crown of your head. Let beauty expand outward, filling the energy fields that wrap around you.

Center yourself in beauty. Let yourself be beautiful now, too.

You are sacred, surrounded by the sacred.

32

CRYSTAL MEDITATION EIGHT

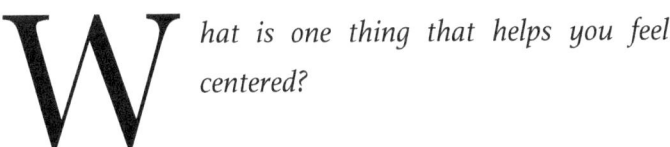

What is one thing that helps you feel centered?

WHAT IS one thing that connects you to stillness inside?

Is it a cluster of tiny purple flowers resting, protected against grey stones? Is it music? Laughter? Is it your meditation or prayer practice? Walking? Reading? Swimming? Resting? Taking a long, slow, deep breath?

For me, it's the small ordinary things that remind me to return to center.

I'm not waiting for the large events, big epiphanies, or vast spiritual openings. I ground myself in the ordinary day to day. That way, my centering becomes constant.

The thing I do almost as automatically is centered breathing and alignment, but this took time. It took years of sitting with myself in sometimes excruciating discomfort for twenty to forty minutes at a time. I had to learn to know myself, you see. To track my patterns. To notice what parts of me wanted to run, and which parts wanted to stay put.

Diligent commitment to those practices formed a solid foundation, so centering is easy for me now.

How about you? What is your current relationship to centering? What helps you? What yanks you off center? What enables you to make a simple return?

Can you make a commitment to the things that help, rather than hinder you?

Breathe in and out. Remember who you are. You can be centered in any moment. You can find refuge and support, like the tiny purple flowers that rest against grey stones.

33

CRYSTAL MEDITATION NINE

We reach higher when we have the support of friends.

THINK OF A STAND OF TREES, rooting deeply, intertwined below the soil, forming community and communicating. Think of their canopies, moving together in the breeze, and providing shelter for birds and animals in hard rain.

Centering is not simply something we do on our own, within ourselves. We center around what we pay attention to. We center around what we give most of our time and energy to. We center around the things that engage our emotional states.

Sometimes, we center around shame, or regret, or fear, or…

And at those times, it is good to recognize that we need outside input. A listening ear. A dance class. A walk and talk. A therapist.

In other words: we need community, be it large or small. And speaking of community, are the friends and family we center our lives around people who feel supportive? Or do they consistently tear us and others down?

We want community that helps us thrive.

The other facet to this is that growth happens in relationship to the world around us. Trees and flowers naturally form groups. Most animals and insects also build and interact in groups.

If you've reached a place in life where you feel stalled out, perhaps what you need is a sounding board, or a challenger, or a few mirrors. Those come in the form of the trustworthy people and beings around us.

In order to reach higher, it is useful to have support around us. No one can go it alone.

At least not for long.

34

CRYSTAL MEDITATION TEN

*hen we approach life with curiosity, we open the way to connection.*

SOMETIMES, to center is to enable the words "I wonder" or "I don't know." When we approach not knowing from a place of curiosity instead of shame or lack, we are able to grow. It also is a sign that we are well centered in ourselves and our lives. There's a generosity in admitting we do not know.

Therefore, centering gives us a chance to learn. Centering gives us the opportunity to explore. We can develop our skills, hone our intuition, expand our awareness of the seen and unseen, deepen our craft, and learn to live well.

If something inside of you resists this, return to the question: "I wonder why I resist this? And what part of me resists?"

There is so much we can uncover through the process of engaging the unknown. Very little in this cosmos is set in stone. Change is the constant. When we challenge our assumptions by saying "I don't know," we encourage a paradigm shift to unfold. And that is some powerful magic.

We cannot will a paradigm shift, but we can encourage it. We can sow the seeds by challenging what we think we collectively know. Things seem set in stone until they are not anymore.

From your most centered place, invoke curiosity.

See what happens.

Something good may be just around the corner.

THE RITUAL OF CENTERING

For this ritual, you will need an object that represents centering to you. It could be a crystal, some incense, a bell, a sun catcher, a flower, or a photo or mandala…let your intuition guide you.

You will also want a candle and a cup of water.

I often like to tidy or clean before doing ritual, allowing the preparation of my space to prepare me internally, as well. This is up to you.

Place your objects together wherever you have clear space. If you have a dedicated working altar, that is perfect. If you don't? Any surface can become a temporary altar space.

Slow your breathing down. Adjust your posture. Relax. Close your eyes for a few moments and just breathe and be.

Next, light your candle. Look at or pick up the object or image that represents centering to you. Breathe with that. Enter into the crystal, bell, incense, flower, or the image....

What does it have to tell you about the power of centering? Let the object whisper to your intuition.

Next, find your own center. In most of us, it rest somewhere between our navel and our pelvic bowl. Inhale. On your next exhalation, allow your attention to drop into your center. Still holding or looking at your object or image, breathe into center for a few moments.

Now, think of your current want, need, or desire around centering. Let this fill you, core outward.

What in your life feels centered? What feels off center?

What is one thing you can do to activate the power of centering in your life, right now?

Lift your object or image and swirl it over the candle flame. Speak that activation out loud. "I will.... I activate the power of Centering."

Set the object back down on the altar. Thank the object. Extinguish the candle. Drink some water. Take some time to simply be.

You are now ready to move into the power of Wishing.

PART V
WISHING

35

DANDELION

The child plucks a dandelion from the ground. Its yellow flower has long shifted into a white puffball, replete with seeds. The child closes their eyes, makes a wish, then blows, scattering the seed pods with their breath, sending their wish upon its way in the hopes that one of those seeds will take root in fertile soil.

To make a wish is an important act of magic. When we wish, we imagine what is possible. We invoke a sense of hope into an often beleaguered world.

To wish is to activate our imaginations. This is an important step toward the manifestation of our dreams and our desires. The ancient Greeks believed that imagination was foundational to all creation. For them, it was a real thing, not something to be passed off as flighty or unimportant.

There is a reason children have such great facility for imagining. They have not yet been trained to think that only the concrete is real.

The thing about wishing, though? It is only one stage on the path of magic and creativity. It is one phase toward manifesting the magic resting in our dreams. This is why the next phase in our magical process is deciding.

Making a decision helps us to take action toward our wishes, large and small.

I sometimes say that fantasy is a great way to try on different hats, to see what they look like and how they feel. But if we spend all of our time in fantasy or wishing without moving toward decision, nothing in our lives will ever change.

We think about what we wish to build.

We center ourselves.

Then we make a wish….

And after wishing, we decide our course of action. And thus our magic continues to unfold.

The world needs visionaries and deep listeners. The world needs people willing to risk the seemingly impossible. All of this begins with imagination and a wish for something more beautiful, equitable, joyous, compassionate, and rich.

36

DANDELION MEDITATION ONE

*e are all we have in this world. Will you reach out a hand?*

WHAT IS your wish for this world? What is your wish for yourself, your communities, your friends? Remember: before we can manifest, we must first imagine what we desire.

We are all we have, friends. In a world on fire, or drowning, or in pain, we are all we have. No one is coming to save us. There is no power on high to intervene. Those of us rooted in this earth like a dandelion flower take small risks each day to connect and stay alive.

Dandelions—like humans—are tenacious. They grow where they are not wanted, in cracks and concrete crevices, or dotting suburban lawns. Dandelions provide food with their nourishing leaves, and splashes of golden joy. Once the yellow flowers have run their course, the plant bursts into seeds anchored to fluffy white parachutes that children—and some adults—wish upon.

Sometimes I think tenacity and stubbornness are the only things keeping us all alive. We keep showing up for life, regardless of how hard it seems, or how alone we may feel.

But the truth is, like the dandelion, we are never truly alone. Together, we form an interdependent whole. Sometimes we're the ones in need, other times it is those around us. And that's what Mutual Aid is all about: we share skills, talents, and resources to keep our communities alive. We offer nourishment and spread new seeds.

And all too often, through creativity and collective effort, communities are able to thrive.

37

DANDELION MEDITATION TWO

Honor that within you that insists upon delight.

Do you hold a wish inside your heart? Is there a bright yellow flower, or a puffball filled with seeds? Does the sense of this delight you? Or are you not in touch with your heart's wishes at all?

How much room do you allow for delight in your life? Is delight reserved for special occasions only? Does it fill you with discomfort, or a sense that you aren't deserving? Or do you allow yourself to glory in the simplest of things, like a dandelion spotted on the side of the road?

Do you wish for delight for yourselves? For your loved ones? For those most downtrodden by our overculture?

Cultivating delight—like nurturing a wish—is important to our healing and our growth. When all we do is grind, hustle, and toil, there is scant room for wishing for anything more, other than in the most exhausted, numbed-out way.

Delight opens the door for wishing. It cracks the carapace that keeps us safe from changes, good or bad.

In order for a seed to grow, its shell must splinter, and it must push up toward sun, wind, and rain. Are you willing to crack your life a bit, to make space for delight? Are you willing to shift routine and open your imagination?

Breathe in. Exhale a wish for delight.

Then allow yourself to be delighted by the smallest things. You just may be surprised.

38

DANDELION MEDITATION THREE

When you call a weed a flower, what might change?

THERE IS SO MUCH in our lives that irritates or interrupts, disturbing our peace and our plans. Can we reframe these? Can we take a breath, center, and approach the irritation or disruption from a different angle?

Sometimes irritation is a sign that life energy is either blocked or running more quickly and faster than we are used to. When we pause, and examine the irritation, we can gather more information. What is our current state trying to tell us? How might we strategize a shift that will feel healthier or less fraught?

In magic, naming is a powerful thing. When we call something an interruption or an irritation, we too often fail to notice that the thing may have other names, as well. Teacher. Ally. Challenger. Herald. A call to pay attention instead of continuing upon our way.

We can see dandelions as weeds to be rooted out and destroyed, but looked at in a different way, we see cheerful flowers, leaves, and stems, filled with vitamins that can be added to summer salads or dried for winter teas.

And when the seed pods appear we can breathe again and imagine ourselves manifesting a wish or two.

When we name a weed a flower, our whole attitude changes. We open to possibility once again.

39

DANDELION MEDITATION FOUR

*S**ome days you greet a faerie door, all spangled, moon and stars....*

ALL CHILDREN ARE animists until they get trained out of it. Some of us never do, remaining connected to the sense that the world is alive and inanimate objects have stories to tell. The world is a place to respect and honor.

There is a glimmering of magic around every corner. There is hope. Possibility. Delight.

Children also have boundless imaginations, until they get trained out of it.

For the ancient Greeks, imagination was so real,

it was foundational. Imagination is the place that every act of creation begins. To wish something into manifest existence, we must first think and dream it into being.

We can expand our imagination by connecting with worlds outside our own. Worlds that feel unknown: The deepest parts of the ocean. The farthest expanse of stars.

A childlike door to faerie set against a tree. A shimmering gateway to the realm of the Powers sometimes called Mystery, or by many other names.

When is the last time you let your imagination guide you somewhere new? Will you make time for magic today?

40

DANDELION MEDITATION FIVE

Do you wish to sink in roots, or wish to fly?

ROOTING AND FLYING ARE, on the surface, opposites.

A tree doesn't fly into the air. Trees take up space, sharing with their companions, staying in one place. But their influence is vast. Trees affect the very air around them, transmuting carbon dioxide and water into food, and then releasing the rest as oxygen. Trees provide shade and shelter. Trees provide homes. And birds carry seeds from trees to places near and far.

Dandelions root into the earth, but when it is

time to spread, they send their seeds off on little parachutes, carried on the backs of animals, or on the soft breath of the breeze.

In other words, sometimes in order to fly, we must first root ourselves. We center, then we wish. We practice, then we wish. The more we have deepened, centered, and stabilized, the farther our wishes can fly. If we never root at all—within ourselves or our communities—it can grow harder and harder to make new seeds at all.

We see this with artists sometimes. If they fail to dig deeper into heart, mind, and soul, their work can become all the same, skimming the surface over time. They are repeating the same wish, over and over, with little result.

The same is true with our magic and our lives. The more we can commit to centering, the more power there is in our wishing.

What will you wish today: Rooting or flying? Or both?

41

DANDELION MEDITATION SIX

Remember that humans have a capacity for wonder.

TIME PASSES. Seas and nations rise and fall. Year follows year as our planet revolves around the sun. The dandelion itself roots and grows, spreads seed, and dies.

The thing that abides is imagination. Wonder. The ability to listen to insects and marvel at their lives. The ability to gaze upon stars and remember how vast our cosmos is, and that we are a part of this earth and this sky.

If we can remember that, we can learn to invoke

change, because change begins with that simple phrase: "I wonder." "I wonder" means, "I don't yet know, but I would like to entertain the possibility."

"I wonder" means, "I am present now, and live in awe at this place where I have landed."

Opening to a sense of wonder helps us to invoke the future, while remaining fully rooted in what is.

What is your relationship with the question "I wonder?" and with wonder itself? Does it feel expansive, or diminished? What might help you to invoke curiosity today?

What is one thing that might help you kindle a sense of awe at this glorious thing called life? Make a wish, and allow it to be so.

42

DANDELION MEDITATION SEVEN

Some beings walk between worlds. Will you meet them?

A FLEETING ENCOUNTER on the train. A message delivered. A bee, buzzing in the garden. The whisper of the wind. A dandelion nodding on the road. Two sticks crossed at your feet. A dream that awakens you in the depth of night.

In your wishing, how aware are you of signs? How often do you pause, breathe, and still yourself inside? How much space do you allow yourself to notice the small messengers that are everywhere?

A kind smile. Pineapple weed growing in a sidewalk crack. A snatch of music. The scent of coming rain. A cat, sauntering to greet you. The trilling of finches. The caw of crows. The feel of paper beneath your fingertips. The warmth of tea in a mug.

The universe communicates to us all the time, if we are open and aware.

In order to wish, we must allow ourselves space to be.

In order to wish, we must remember we are part of this world, and in relationship with it.

When we remember, every moment fills with possibility.

What do you notice, right now? What is trying to tell you something?

Are you open to the message as and when it arrives?

Keep breathing.

43

DANDELION MEDITATION EIGHT

The path is never certain. Keep seeking what you desire.

SOMETIMES WE WONDER what the use of wishing is. We try and try and the outcome is never what we imagined it to be.

That's the point. The future never looks or feels the way we imagined it would. Why is that? Because the path itself is uncertain. It is not only uncertain because we cannot ascertain every turn and twist. The path is uncertain because we co-create the future with the path.

We co-create the future—and the past and present—with everything around us.

We show up, wishes in tow. We do our best. We make an effort. We continue to wish and to strive.

The dandelion grows, not knowing if its seeds will spread anywhere at all. The dandelion sprouts and strives toward rain and sunlight no matter what conditions it finds itself in.

The dandelion seed was planted from a wish from the season before. Perhaps it was carried someplace strange and far away. The new plant grows where it was planted.

We can do the same.

When we divorce ourselves from attachment to the outcome of desire, we can adjust with the path as it winds. And all too often, if we pause and take a breath?

We might just find we've ended up in a place that is better than the one we were wishing for.

44

DANDELION MEDITATION NINE

hen you thought about giving up, you bloomed again, creating new seeds.

It is easy to give up.

It is hard to give up.

Both of these statements are true. But whether we cling to our hopes or release them far too soon, we have the opportunity to make space for something new.

In my own life, I have crashed, hard, and taken to my bed with burnout. This led me down a path I'd abandoned long before. It led me into deeper, brighter magic, and the great satisfaction of a tale well told.

I had planted seeds decades before, and given them up as an impractical wish. Well, guess what? Because I was forced to give up something else, those seeds came roaring back, and grew into a glorious field of flowers.

When we continue to wish, even on the verge of giving up, when we surrender to the moment and the deeper wisdom of body, soul, heart, and mind, new possibilities spring up around us.

This process may take time. The field may need to lay fallow for awhile. We may need to rest and regroup. All of that is part of the process, too.

Our wishes are never fully abandoned. Sometimes they need to gestate beneath the soil, then be tended a bit.

Sometimes we need to give ourselves and our dreams another chance.

45

DANDELION MEDITATION TEN

ishing you new growth under gentle conditions.

SOMETIMES WE THINK we need to work full out to achieve what we desire. Sometimes that is even true.

Sometimes we think we don't deserve the things we wish for. What can help us shift this thinking around?

Hard work can feel satisfying. I love nothing more than being filled with energy and verve, and getting good things done. But other times? I just need a break. If I'm truly listening to myself, and am not simply facing my own resistance to change, I can recognize that I need to slow down. To push when I truly need to rest means I risk breaking the project or myself. At the very least, my work will be done in a state of diminishing returns, and will likely need to be redone again tomorrow.

What would life be like if we wished for gentler conditions? If we wished for support? If we wished for ease and flexibility?

What would life be like if we did not punish ourselves and others?

We might be able to turn our faces toward a gentle breeze, and take a breath. We might be able to grow in ways that feel healthier, less grueling, and less toxic.

What might life be like if we could live as healthy and whole human beings on this beloved planet? What then?

Isn't that a lovely wish to cultivate?

In the meantime, here's wishing you just the right challenge.

Here's wishing you strength and ease.

46

THE RITUAL OF WISHING

For this ritual, you will need an object that represents wishing to you. It could be a dandelion, a child's magic wand, a star, or a photo or piece of art...let your intuition guide you.

You will also want a candle and a cup of water.

I often like to tidy or clean before doing ritual, allowing the preparation of my space to prepare me internally, as well. This is up to you.

Place your objects together wherever you have clear space. If you have a dedicated working altar, that is perfect. If you don't? Any surface can become a temporary altar space.

Slow your breathing down. Adjust your posture. Relax. Close your eyes for a few moments and just breathe and be.

Next, light your candle. Look at or pick up the object or image that represents wishing to you. Breathe with that. Enter into the dandelion, magic wand, star, or the image....

What does it have to tell you about the power of wishing? Let the object whisper to your intuition.

Next, drop into your center, and ask yourself, "What do I wish?"

Now, think of your current want, need, or desire around this wish. Let this fill you, from your center outward.

What in your life feels excited by this wish? What longs for it? What feels afraid? Just be and breathe, feeling the power of your wish expanding.

What is one thing you can do to activate the power of wishing in your life, right now?

Lift your object or image and swirl it over the candle flame. Speak that activation out loud. "I will.... I activate the power of my Wish."

Set the object back down on the altar. Thank the object. Extinguish the candle. Drink some water. Take some time to simply be.

You are now ready to move into the power of Deciding.

PART VI
DECIDING

47

BLADE

The power to choose is available to us in every moment if we remember it. Too often, we feel we have no choices. And certainly, many facets of life are out of our direct control.

But we can choose to focus in each moment on the things we can do or not do, the words we can say or not say. We can focus on our emotions and notice what they are trying to tell us. We can root in our bodies to deepen our connection instead of flying off into further states of disconnection.

It sounds simple, right? And it is, through steady practice. I liken making choices to walking a blade. For me, this is the classic witch's athame, with two sharp edges and a point.

As I hold this tool of discernment in my hand, I also imagine it stretched out on the floor in front of me, with my body at the hilt.

Try it.

Then imagine moving down the middle: a yes on the left, a no on your right. Or two separate things that you need to choose between this day. Feel the push and pull of the choices on either side of you. Then, when you reach the tip, allow your consciousness to balance there. Yes and no, left and right, this or that...they all come together at this point.

The tip of the blade is the third option. We can choose something completely different here, or we can choose to *not* choose one thing or another. Perhaps we need more time. More information. Deeper discernment.

Moving back to the hilt, we allow our consciousness to step off the blade. Feeling the knife in our hands, we can cut away one side or another, or point toward the tip, choosing the energy of the place where yes and no join as one.

We hold within ourselves the power of yes and no. We also hold that power to remain with both.

In every moment, we are surrounded by choices, large and small. Sometimes the choices are external, but most often, there are inner adjustments we can make to thought, feeling, or expression.

We get to decide what we choose.

48

BLADE MEDITATION ONE

*here light meets shadow, beauty dwells.*

THE CLASSIC MAGICAL blade has two edges that meet to form a whole.

Life is lived in the contrasts revealed by each side of the blade. Both light and shadow help us find the texture of our lives. Light too bright or noise too loud washes out everything, and the intensity can cause us to cringe.

We need variation for all of our senses—and for our hearts and minds—in order to make sense of the world. If we are always running or always staying still, we miss out on the subtle flow of information that helps us choose the lives we truly want to live.

What are you ignoring? What are you taking in? What do you reject or accept? Do these need to be reexamined?

What do you notice about the texture of your life? Does it feel rich and satisfying? Does it feel static or impoverished?

What do you desire? And what will you choose to do about it?

You hold the blade, with its two edges coming to a point. You can choose what you decide. Right here. Right now.

49

BLADE MEDITATION TWO

Into the coming storms, take flight.

I LOVE WATCHING my neighborhood crows.

Crows teach us to soar as clouds gather. They teach us to work together to face what is to come. We cannot know the outcome or severity of the storm, but together, we can live through it. We can take a risk and fly.

This choice to fly is a decision, because every risk requires a decision. Remaining still is as much of a risk as taking flight. Not deciding is a decision.

The power of the blade cuts through the indecision: to fly or not to fly. To brave the storm or to take shelter. There is no right or wrong decision because all decisions come from active relationship.

If I am in active relationship to the coming storm —be it physical, mental, or emotional—I can better choose whether I need to fly with the storm, run from the storm, confront the storm, or shelter from the storm.

The crows fly into a storm that is on its way, getting last things done before the deluge hits. They take care of their families, making sure they are as safe as possible. Only then do they shelter.

What is right for you, in this moment? What are the storms around you?

What action—or inaction—will you choose?

50

BLADE MEDITATION THREE

Drink some water. Get some rest. Don't give up.

WE THINK of blades as fierce tools, and they can be. But they can also be homely, practical tools. Blades can be used to protect our boundaries. Blades can also remind us of the simpler boundaries, close to home. A choice to pick up the blade to chop some vegetables for a nourishing dinner. A boundary to not overexert ourselves. A boundary to remember our internal blade and protect our meditation or art time from interruption. The reminder that in order to commit to the long haul, we may need to step back for a moment or two, or sometimes even a few years.

Drink water. Get rest. Don't give up.

All of these are decisions. These are decisions to care for ourselves and decisions to stay alive. This helps us to better choose when to engage. And when to choose a world worth fighting for.

How are you wielding your blade of decision today? Are you making choices to help you toward long-term sustainable action? Are you taking care of the small stuff so you have better support when dealing with the large?

Remember: every moment of every day, we have a choice.

Today, you are called upon to choose the things you need. To choose what is foundational to your well-being.

Don't worry, the big stuff will still be there when you return. Or perhaps someone else will have shouldered the burden while you were gone.

51

BLADE MEDITATION FOUR

*usps are filled with the magic of possibility.*

LIMINAL SPACES ARE PERMEABLE BOUNDARIES. When a witch draws a circle with their blade, they mark a separate, in-between space. Neither here nor there. Neither in time nor outside of time.

Liminal spaces unlock the magic of attention and intention. The meeting of contrasts becomes the ground of creativity.

I like liminal spaces. Dusk. Dawn. Thresholds of all sorts. The thing I like most about thresholds is that you pass through them.

Thresholds are, by their nature, temporary, shifting states. Reminders that the way humans mark both time and space is a construct. Even mountains are in flux. It's just hard for us—so much shorter-lived—to tell.

Pushing through thresholds and delighting in liminal spaces is part of my nature, and likely one of the things that draws me toward magic. What is your relationship to thresholds and cusps? Do you wish to stay with them or get through as quickly as possible?

Some of us feel liminal ourselves, as if we never really fit in here or there. Realizing this helped me to pick up my blade and decide I may as well be myself.

Approaching a cusp gives us the opportunity to decide what makes sense to us, heart, body, and soul.

For me? When I picked up my blade, I decided to glory in the gloaming. To dance at the edges. I embraced the witches, the artists, the queers, and the crows. All of those things that skirted the edges of the known and acceptable worlds became my allies. And that has made so much magic possible.

What threshold are you approaching? What does that magic feel like? Will you choose to stay here for a while, or will you rush on through?

And what are some of the things that make up who you are?

What are some of the things you want to choose?

52

BLADE MEDITATION FIVE

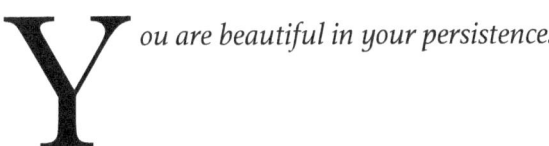

You are beautiful in your persistence.

When life feels hard, or tedious, or heartbreaking, or overwhelming, how do you find it in yourself to keep going? What do you decide is important enough to try, no matter what? Some people manage to persist through war, abuse, illness, and many other hardships. Some people manage to persist when things are comfortable, and everything seems to be going their way.

Other people don't, in both situations. For some, hardship is a goad and comfort can lead to complacency. For others, it is the opposite: hardship makes doing much of anything impossible, and comfort helps them thrive.

Which are you? It is good to know ourselves and know what support we need in order to decide to keep showing up for what we want, need, and desire.

How do we find a balance for ourselves that feels healthy? When do we need to pick up the blade and cut something away? When do we need to choose one thing or another?

Take a breath and drop more deeply into your center. Inhale. Pause. Exhale. Pause. Inhale…

In order to persist, we cannot carry everything with us. Some burdens are too heavy, or simply are not ours to carry.

Imagine a magical blade in your hand. What will you choose today, to support your persistence? And what will you allow to fall away?

53

BLADE MEDITATION SIX

Some days, your strange, fierce, gorgeous self roars a song into the sky.

SOMETIMES THE BLADE is a practical and homely tool. Other times the blade reminds us of our fierce sides.

Have you decided to live fully as yourself? Or as fully as you can right now? And if you cannot yet live fully, are there any actions you can take to begin manifesting a greater sense of safety, or bravery, or whatever else you need?

Whatever your current conditions are, let this phrase remind you that somewhere inside of you is a strange, fierce, gorgeous being, ready to roar. You decide that for yourself, no one else. You decide when you are ready, no one else.

What stops you from roaring out your song?

What keeps you from roaring out your beauty or your pain? What is kindled inside of you, longing to be free to roar?

Breathe into your center. Imagine a blade held firmly in your hand. Feel the power of earth beneath your feet and the power of sky surrounding you. Adjust your spine. Find a posture that makes you feel powerful and seen.

Lift your blade to the sky and speak your truth into the world.

Shout your truth. Scream and sing and roar your truth. Lift your blade and live.

54

BLADE MEDITATION SEVEN

Be Bright! the hawthorn flowers say, But don't forget your thorns.

WE ARE PART OF NATURE, and nature reminds us that beauty and strength go hand in hand. This is another time that we must choose: to be visible, as ourselves, but to not take abuse.

Like tiny blades, the thorns of the hawthorn tree provide protection. The spring flowers are soft and inviting, and the winter fruit stark and red, offering food. In both of these stages of the tree, the thorns remain. We can be soft and hold a boundary. We can be nurturing and fierce.

Softness is not an invitation to be mistreated or taken advantage of. The softer we are, the stronger we can become. There is strength in vulnerability when it is done by choice. There is strength in nurturing when we wish to give.

Meditate on the hawthorn tree today. Imagine its soft flowers—five petals, white or pink—bright and bursting in the spring. Imagine its berries, glowing red in the winter's darkness. Imagine the long thorns, protecting every branch.

What if you were that tree? How would that feel?

BLADE MEDITATION EIGHT

Can we learn to set boundaries without shutting out the whole world?

A HUMMINGBIRD SITS ATOP A TREE. In some Indigenous cultures, hummingbirds are magic, appearing and disappearing in a flash, feathers reflecting the light of the sun.

Hummingbirds are fierce. Solitary. Territorial. They remind me of tiny warriors, with their blade-sharp beaks. Those beaks, designed to sip nectar from flowers, become weapons in a fight. The thing that helps the bird take in sustenance is the very thing it uses to defend access to the flowers.

We humans also have needs. Sometimes we have to fight to get those needs met. Sometimes fighting becomes a habit that is hard to break. Once solitary, how do we trust? How do we learn to share space? And how do we learn to set boundaries while not using those same boundaries to shut out the rest of the world?

How do we claim space for art, music, work, or our mental, emotional, or physical health, while acknowledging that we might want to share space later on? And conversely, how do we come to comprehend our own worth so that someone else's boundary doesn't feel like rejection?

Some days, we need to become like a hummingbird, and fight for our boundaries. Other times? Perhaps we fought too soon, turning away a chance to connect on a deeper level.

There is conflict in life, and there are flowers. There are times for a sense of satisfaction and contentment in being solitary, and times to choose connection once again.

Protect your boundaries if you need to. But don't forget to sheath your blade sometimes, and reach out, too.

BLADE MEDITATION NINE

Take a breath and shift perspective.

SHIFTING PERSPECTIVE IS A CHOICE. Just as a blade is forged in fire, the fire is fed by wood and air. Sometimes we are so deeply in the weeds of our lives, we cannot perceive anything not directly in front of us. Sometimes we cannot even perceive anything outside of ourselves.

When we find ourselves in this state, it is time to pick up the blade again and choose to shift our hearing, our vision, our thinking, or our feeling. Perhaps after that shift in perspective, we'll find we need to return to where we were. But we may just find a bit of magic waiting for us elsewhere.

To choose to shift perspective requires practice. This is where having a daily touchstone offers assistance. We need a daily prayer or meditation practice, or a daily walk, or oracle card pull, or a physical practice that reminds us there is more to life than living in the weeds.

There's a whole world living around and with us, should we choose to acknowledge it.

When we can focus on a task or situation at hand, while retaining awareness of the world, we can work more powerful magic than before.

What will you decide today? How will you shift your perspective and deepen your understanding?

BLADE MEDITATION TEN

The fire lives deep inside the blade.

A BLADE IS FORGED in the heat of the fire. It is pounded and shaped and heated once again. The blade must grow soft in order to grow strong and resilient once again. The fire that softens the metal for forging lives on in the blade.

The same fire lives within us. The fire of life softens and forges us, tempering us and making us either brittle or strong. Sometimes we must return to the fire to soften ourselves again. Other times, the fire is a test of our mettle.

Mettle is a variant of the word metal and has come to mean our inner strength. Mettle is our ability to make it through hard times and challenges. Strong mettle carries us through the forge of life.

What is your current relationship to your inner fire? Are you choosing to cultivate the spark of creation? The flame of magic? The warmth of home?

How is your mettle? Do you feel strong or brittle? What might soften you awhile, so you can come back stronger in the future?

Will you share your fire with the world?

58

THE RITUAL OF DECIDING

For this ritual, you will need an object that represents deciding to you. It could be a blade, a set of scales, a checkerboard, or a photo or piece of art…let your intuition guide you.

You will also want a candle and a cup of water.

I often like to tidy or clean before doing ritual, allowing the preparation of my space to prepare me internally, as well. This is up to you.

Place your objects together wherever you have clear space. If you have a dedicated working altar, that is perfect. If you don't? Any surface can become a temporary altar space.

Slow your breathing down. Adjust your posture. Relax. Close your eyes for a few moments and just breathe and be.

Next, light your candle. Look at or pick up the object or image that represents deciding to you. Breathe with that. Enter into the blade, the scales, the checkerboard, or the image....

What does it have to tell you about the power of deciding? Let the object whisper to your intuition.

Next, drop into your center, call up your wish if you have one, and ask yourself, "What do I will? What shall I decide?"

Now, think of your current want, need, or desire around your wish, or around a current situation that requires a decision.

Then call upon the power you have to decide. The power to say yes, no, or to gather more information. Let this power fill you from your center outward.

How does it feel in your body, heart, soul, and mind, to have the power to Decide?

What is one thing you can do to activate the power of deciding in your life, right now?

Lift your object or image and swirl it over the candle flame. Speak that activation out loud. "I will.... I activate the power to Decide."

Set the object back down on the altar. Thank the object. Extinguish the candle. Drink some water. Take some time to simply be.

You are now ready to move into the power of Manifesting.

PART VII
MANIFESTING

BEE

Bees create hives together. They collectively gather pollen and help flowers and food to grow. Together, they make honey and feed their community.

Bees manifest a world through collective action.

We have moved from building, to centering, to wishing, to deciding. It is now time to manifest.

I'd like to offer seven steps toward manifestation:

ONE—WHAT is your current dominant emotional state? Fear? Anger? Excitement? Joy? Love? Defeat? Grief? Ambition? Interest? Awe?

Two—Breathe into that dominant emotion. Expand around it. Give it space.

Three—What is at the root of that emotion? What's the first thing that comes to mind?

If it's fear, what are you most afraid of? If it's anger, what are you most angry about? If it's excitement, what are you most excited about? If it's love, what are you most in love with?

Whatever the dominant emotion is, get to the root and write that down.

Four—What can you build from the kernel at the heart of that dominant emotion? How can that spur you on?

Five—What is the first or next action you can take toward manifesting what you desire? Write that down. Does it feel too big? Too daunting? Too terrifying?

Look at it again. Can it be broken into even smaller actions? Or does something need to happen alongside your main next action? Maybe you need to learn to act *and* learn to call a therapist. Maybe you need to learn to act *and* get more training.

We don't need to wait until things feel perfectly ready, or we feel perfectly healed, in order to manifest what we desire. We learn as we go. We make mistakes, repeatedly, and if we persist? We grow.

Six—Figure out what else you need as you take

that first action. Gather resources, friends, or education.

Seven—Keep going. Don't let failure—or the fear of it—stop you.

TAKE what is at the heart of you and act.

Keep breathing. Keep reassessing. As soon as we act, the future changes, and therefore so does our goal. Our task is to remain present and adaptable.

Our task is to continue to try.

60

BEE MEDITATION ONE

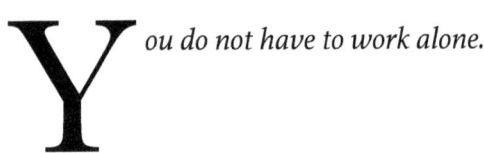

Y*ou do not have to work alone.*

REMEMBER the collective creativity of bees.

We often think that in order to manifest something, we have to use only our will, our resources, and our time. The reality is that we co-create everything. Nothing springs fully formed from our heads like Athena from the brow of Zeus.

Every conversation, every walk, every lunch bought, every chance given, every class taken, every book read and song listened to, every leaf fall, every storm...all of these come together to help us manifest what we desire in the present moment.

As interdependent beings, we manifest along with the whole cosmos. Even when we feel alone in our quest, we are supported by all sorts of tiny things. The people who picked or delivered the food we eat. The flower that brightened our day. The job that helps us pay our rent.

To begin the work of manifestation, let's start with gratitude, today. What is one thing you may notice all the time, or one thing you may take for granted? Can you inhale, exhale, and feel gratitude for that?

The more gratitude we cultivate for the support —large or small—we have in our lives, the more easily manifestation will come.

Trying to go it all alone can make things harder. Let's pause to acknowledge that the world is conspiring to help us.

What do you feel grateful for today?

BEE MEDITATION TWO

*P**rotect your light, but shine on anyway.*

WHEN WE BEGIN concentrated work on manifesting our desires, sometimes people come out to help and cheer us on.

Others may wish to steal or squash the light inside our hearts, spirits, and minds because of ignorance, jealousy, fear, or hatred. We can protect our light. We can choose where and when to share it.

But we cannot let others extinguish that light.

It is our purpose to share our light with the world.

It is part of our purpose to become luminous.

This often requires examining what has been hidden in our lives. There is purpose and growth in our darkness, too. There is mystery there. Sometimes it takes years—even decades—for that mystery to unfold. When we learn to plumb the darkness and embrace the light, we shine even more brightly than before.

When we fear the darkness, we can remember the moon. We can remember the light in our hearts. We can recall the beauty of midnight, and the hush of the earth.

The things we hide from others? Usually, they are not so terrifying. And if they are, we can get help.

Learning to claim our darkness is the best way to protect our light. We no longer fear exposure at the hands of those who would hurt us.

We can shine in the full knowledge of who and what we are.

62

BEE MEDITATION THREE

Be present in the midst of change, invoke a light heart and an open mind.

CHANGE CAN FEEL FRIGHTENING. It asks us to reach beyond the status quo. But nothing new is brought to life without changing the current order of things. Every risk requires change.

How do we navigate our resistance to manifesting something different? We examine our lives. We question our attitudes. We practice being present in discomfort and in comfort, in boredom and excitement, in sorrow and in joy.

When we breathe into our hearts, we invoke the

lightness of the bee. When we exhale, we can open our minds to change.

When you imagine the life you desire, what is your list of requirements? Is there any flexibility in that list? How much space have you allowed for the universe to move with you?

Remember, while it is good to be committed to our lives, we are not wholly in control. Does that frighten you, or feel liberating? Breathe into whatever that emotion is. As you exhale, feel your energy expand. Do this two more times if you need to.

From that more expansive place, invoke a light heart and an open mind. Then prepare for the next action toward manifesting what you desire.

BEE MEDITATION FOUR

If we allow ourselves to bloom, the world is better.

FLOWERS FEED THE BEES. Bees feed the flowers. All of nature is engaged in the symbiotic dance of life.

We tend the garden of heart, mind, body, and soul. We tend to community, family, and friends.

When we release ourselves from the covering safety of rich, dark soil, we rise to sunlight, to stars at night, to wind and rain and all the changes that life brings.

We carry the memory of the soil and the cradling darkness. We carry the memory of feeling cocooned.

Held. We carry the memory of the struggle to crack the shell and venture into the unknown.

We carry the memory of the first taste of a new world.

With all of that inside us, how can we not manifest the world that we desire? With that amount of flexibility, perseverance, strength, and daring, how can we do anything but succeed?

What are three things you want or need right now to help you toward success? Write those down.

Then pick one, take a breath, and begin....

64

BEE MEDITATION FIVE

Be the tiny pollinator you want to see in the world.

LISTEN to the gentle buzzing of the bees at work. See their lightness as they move from plant to plant. Notice when they rest. When they pause to drink some water, cupped inside a leaf. Notice the sunlight on their wings.

You can be a pollinator, too. Collecting information and insights. Floating from thing to thing, alighting softly. Staying awhile. Then moving on.

There is nothing that says the work of manifestation has to always feel hard. Oh, sometimes it might, and we do need to put in effort, but sometimes lightening up is exactly what we need.

What would it feel like to hold your desires and ambitions lightly, inside cupped palms, instead of gripping them as tightly as you can, expending the greatest amount of effort possible?

What would it feel like if what you are manifesting helps others manifest, too? When we move closer to living the lives that we desire, everything around us is helped by that. Some relationships may fall away, but others will deepen.

We may even inspire someone without knowing it. They might hear or see what we're doing and think to themselves, "Maybe I can manifest what I desire, too."

Take a risk today and lighten up. Imagine yourself as a bee, moving from flower to flower. See what happens.

Breathe.

BEE MEDITATION SIX

Wealth comes in many forms. Here's to the wealth that feeds us, heart, body, and soul.

WHAT IS TRULY important to you? How much is your life focused around that?

Gratitude practice is a way of centering ourselves in what we truly wish to manifest. Gratitude reminds me of the wealth that I already have. This doesn't mean I don't still strive: to create, to serve, to live a healthier life, to share love.... But I also already have a lot of those things.

I just said that gratitude practice helps us center in what we truly wish to manifest. But that is not all.

The practice of gratitude is a manifestation practice in and of itself. In noticing what I have, it becomes easier to make space for more.

If we are always coming from a place of lack, it can be hard to unclench ourselves enough to let what we desire move into our lives.

That's why I'm wishing us all wealth that really feeds us, and our families, friends, and communities.

I also wish for us all the ability to recognize and thank that wealth when it arrives.

In what ways have you already manifested what you desire? What is the wealth that surrounds you, right now? What do you have in excess, that you can offer to others?

And how does examining these questions help you refine what you will move toward next?

BEE MEDITATION SEVEN

Something new and beautiful is on the way.

DROP INTO YOUR CENTER. Breathe. Now, place one hand on your heart, and one hand somewhere around your navel. Imagine a crescent moon, traced upon your forehead. Inhale the magic of that sliver of light. Allow it to trace the edges of your body.

Imagine a bee, lighting on a flower, reminding you that beauty exists in the simplest moment.

From this place, say a prayer or light a candle with the intention that you be open to something new and beautiful. Something unexpected that will offer you a gift your heart and soul may have wanted but never knew to ask for.

Imagine the pathway opening to you, lit by the light of the moon and the dance of the bee. Does this path lead toward you, paving the way for the good things to come? Or is the pathway there to draw you on toward the glimmering of newness in the distance?

Listen from your center. Is something about to arrive, or are you about to move to meet it?

Either way, remain open to the beauty arriving in your life. You are magic.

BEE MEDITATION EIGHT

Love this life to the best of your abilities, for as long as you can.

TO CONSISTENTLY MANIFEST what we desire requires a measure of love. If we are always making magic from a place of lack, it can become harder and harder to attract anything that will fill our hearts and souls.

This reality only increases when we strive to manifest things for our communities, large or small. There are multiple sayings about fighting for what we love instead of fighting against what we hate.

Why? Because we can only fight against something for so long. If all of our energy is tied up in the negative, that leaves little space for the positive. It leaves little room for wishing and deciding, for imagining the power of what could be.

The better able we are to center ourselves in what we love, the more sustainable our actions become, and the more our desires slot into alignment with our lives.

The more aligned we are, the stronger our ability to manifest becomes.

So, what do you love today? It need not be something large. Answer the question of what you love and find one way to act from that space.

Manifestation will grow easier and easier over time.

BEE MEDITATION NINE

*eet me where the moss greets the pavement. We'll make some magic there.*

WE MANIFEST where and when we can. We make our magic in the eternal now. We live in the cracks and crevices as well as in the open air. There is no place we do not belong, if we desire it badly enough.

From a centered place, where we have decided to trust and choose ourselves, that is where true desire arises. When we are aligned in our lives and with our will, we manifest what is meant to be.

If we can imagine it, we can choose it. If we can choose it—from a place of centered alignment—we can build the dream into being. This is true for our individual endeavors, and even more so from our communal desires.

Imagine now, the communities you wish to thrive among. Imagine justice, joy, and creative freedom. Imagine yourself, happy in the midst of it all, challenged well, and supported by the life that surrounds you.

We can make magic from the edges, as outcasts and dreamers. We can make magic from the center, as priests of the sacred ways. We notice the moss meeting the pavement. We honor the moss, and the pavement, and the crooked line where soft touches hard.

We hold all duality within our hands.

We speak the worlds anew.

Can you feel it? If you can, then take a risk.

If you can't yet? Touch the moss and the pavement and ask them to teach you how.

BEE MEDITATION TEN

To manifest what you desire, take what is at the heart of you, and act.

MANIFESTATION REQUIRES WILL, breath, and desire. Manifestation requires years of getting to know the self and the world. Manifestation requires effort.

Manifestation is easy. All we have to do is bring heart and soul and mind into alignment. How do we do that? We practice, every day. Simple. We show up for ourselves and our communities. Simple.

None of this starts off as simple, of course. None of this starts off as easy. But over the years, as we choose to practice, again and again, building, centering, aligning, wishing, deciding, choosing...it all becomes as simple as can be. How?

We know our practices and they help us know ourselves. We know our practices and they help us know our friends, families, and communities. We know our practices and they help us know this earth, and the vast cosmos beyond.

Once we allow things to become simple, they also become easy. Does our magic still require effort? Yes, but not as much as before. The days and years of practice form the strongest foundation anything has ever been built upon.

All we have to do in this state is to listen to our hearts, choose, and act.

Simple. Let it be simple.

Just be.

THE RITUAL OF MANIFESTATION

For this ritual, you will need an object that represents manifestation to you. It could be a bowl of berries, some money, a heart sculpture, a jar of honey, or a photo or piece of art... let your intuition guide you.

You will also want a candle and a cup of water and a journal or paper and pen.

I often like to tidy or clean before doing ritual, allowing the preparation of my space to prepare me internally, as well. This is up to you.

Place your objects together wherever you have clear space. If you have a dedicated working altar, that is perfect. If you don't? Any surface can become a temporary altar space.

Slow your breathing down. Adjust your posture.

Relax. Close your eyes for a few moments and just breathe and be.

Next, light your candle. Look at or pick up the object or image that represents manifestation to you. Breathe with that. Enter into the berries, the money, the honey, the heart, or the image....

What does it have to tell you about the power of manifestation? Let the object whisper to your intuition.

Next, drop into your center and ask yourself, "Am I willing to manifest my desire?"

Now, think of your current want, need, or desire around something you wish to manifest, large or small.

Then call upon the power inside you. The power to decide and then set intention into action. This is your will, your ability to do in this world. Let this power fill you from your center outward.

How does it feel in your body, heart, soul, and mind, to have the power to Manifest?

What is one thing you can do to activate the power of manifestation in your life, right now?

Lift your object or image and swirl it over the candle flame. Speak that activation out loud. "I will.... I activate the power to Manifest what I want, need, and desire."

Set the object back down on the altar. Thank the object. Extinguish the candle. Drink some water. Take some time to simply be.

You are now ready to manifest.

Open your journal. Write down some steps needed to manifest your desire. Breathe with those steps. Then circle or highlight the next action you commit to. Make time to engage with that action this week.

Blessed be.

PART VIII
CLOSING

71

THE CYCLE CONTINUES

The world's alight
With beauty's flame.
Your own spark shines within.

THERE IS no end to the cycle of building, centering, deciding, wishing, and manifesting. We are all at different phases of this cycle in our lives. And we may be in a building portion in one area of life, and a wishing or deciding phase in yet another. That is fine. What matters is continuously returning to active relationship with all parts of ourselves and our lives. What matters is continuously remembering we are in relationship, not only with friends, family, or communities, but with the land, sea, sky, and stars.

We are also in relationship with magic.

My desire for you is this:

May you remember your connection to magic, every day. May you manifest the life and world that you desire.

Wishing you safety, courage, love, comfort, strength, prosperity, community, and joy.

THANK YOU

I am so grateful to my Kickstarter and Patreon backers without whom this book would not exist.

Thanks also to everyone who chimes in on my weekly newsletter, my social media, and blog posts, letting me know when my words and images resonate. Because of you, this book began...

Thanks also to Leslie Claire Walker and Jack, my first readers, and to Dayle Dermatis who edited this book. Immense gratitude to Jonathan Korman for last minute formatting help. And this whole project —book and oracle deck—has been greatly enhanced by Maxine Miller's amazing artwork.

Thanks as always to my household for continuous cheerleading and support.

The magic of writing shifts and changes over time.

You are all part of that.

May your magic help to re-enchant this world.

I wish you all the best.

T. Thorn Coyle
Portland, OR, 2023

REVIEWS

Reviews are always appreciated! If you enjoyed this book, please tell a friend.
If you want to get weekly musings from Thorn in your inbox, please visit thorncoyle.com

ABOUT THE AUTHOR

T. Thorn Coyle worked in many strange and diverse occupations before settling in to write books. A queer, nonbinary mystic, Thorn has been a student of the magical arts for forty years and taught in nine countries, on four continents, and in twenty-five states.

Author of the *Seashell Cove Paranormal Mystery* series, the *Pride Street Paranormal Cozy Mysteries*, *The Steel Clan Saga*, *The Witches of Portland*, and *The Panther Chronicles*, Thorn's multiple non-fiction books include *Sigil Magic for Writers, Artists & Other Creatives*, *Kissing the Limitless, Make Magic of Your Life,* and *Evolutionary Witchcraft.* Thorn's work also appears in many anthologies, magazines, and collections.

An interloper to the Pacific Northwest U.S., Thorn drinks a lot of tea, pays proper tribute to the neighborhood cats, and talks to crows, squirrels, and trees.

Connect with Thorn:
www.thorncoyle.com

ALSO BY T. THORN COYLE

FICTION

Seashell Cove Paranormal Cozy Mysteries

Bookshop Witch

Haunted Witch

Tarot Witch

Running Witch

Hallows Witch

Solstice Witch

The Pride Street Paranormal Cozy Mysteries

Sushi Scandal

Flower Frenzy

Muffin Murder

The Witches of Portland (complete)

By Earth

By Flame

By Wind

By Sea

By Moon

By Sun

By Dusk

By Dark

By Witch's Mark

The Panther Chronicles (Complete)

To Raise a Clenched Fist to the Sky

To Wrest Our Bodies From the Fire

To Drown This Fury in the Sea

To Stand With Power on This Ground

The Steel Clan Saga

We Seek No Kings

We Heed No Laws

We Ride at Night

Short Story Collections

A Hint of Faery

A Touch of Faery

A Spark of Magic

A Flame for Yuletide

A Hope for Winter

A Time for Magic

A Speculation of Stars

A Speculation of Hope

A Speculation of Time

Risk It All: Queer Stories of Love, Suspense, And Daring

Thresholds: Queer Stories of Love, Suspense, And Daring

Cats and Other Creatures

NON-FICTION

Evolutionary Witchcraft

Kissing the Limitless

Make Magic of Your Life

Sigil Magic for Writers, Artists & Other Creatives

Crafting a Daily Practice

Resistance Matters

www.ingramcontent.com/pod-product-compliance
Lightning Source LLC
Chambersburg PA
CBHW070141080526
44586CB00015B/1783